Thank You for This Child

Prayer Thoughts for Parents

Jeanette L. Groth

Illustrations by Gordon Willman

Publishing House
St. Louis

This book may not be reproduced in whole or in part, by mimeograph or any other means, without permission. For information address: Concordia Publishing House, St. Louis, MO 63118.

All rights reserved
Copyright © 1980 by Concordia Publishing House

Library of Congress Cataloging in Publication Data

Groth, Jeanette L   1947-
    Thank You for This Child
    1. Family—Prayer-books and devotions—English.   I. Title.
BV4845.G76   242'.84   79-20170
ISBN 0-570-03797-2

To our children, with many prayers that God will always keep them close to Him.

Contents

Foreword	7
SPECIAL DAYS	8
A Sunny Day	8
First Day of School	8
A Baptism	10
Birthday	10
Advent	12
Christmas	12
Valentines	14
Easter	14
First Day of Sunday School	17
A Spring Day	17
SPECIAL NEEDS	18
Forgiveness	18
Illness	18
Illness	20
Counsel	20
Patience	22
Waiting	22

THE WORLD AROUND US	25
Vacation	25
The Park	25
Snow	27
The Zoo	27
The Fish	29
THANKS FOR . . .	30
Returned Health	30
Jesus Picture	30
Skills	33
Simple Gifts	33
Growth	35
DAILY SITUATIONS	37
Bath Time	37
Family Devotions	37
Nap Time	38
A Child's Dance	38
Disciplining	41
Hiding	41
Question	42
TV Viewing	42
Favorite Shows	44
Supper	44
Disagreements	46

Hunger	46
Devotions	49
Prayer	49
Love	50
Family	50
The Haircut	53
Daddy Is Gone	53
Playing House	55
The Funeral	55

COMMON OBJECTS 56

Crayons	56
Toys	56
That Blanket	59
The Mirror	59
The Mailbox	61
A Siren	61
The Wall	63

Foreword

"Pray without ceasing" (1 Thess. 5:17) sets a high and noble goal before every child of God. But how does a harried parent do this when eager, active children are needing constant love and attention? Perhaps the answer comes in training the heart and mind to see each unfolding situation as a chance to share our Savior's love with the children in our care, as well as an opportunity for us to tune ourselves into the wonderful will and ways of our God. Then the commonplace holds new purpose, the drudgeries change to joys, and the high points of life take on a whole new dimension.

It is my prayer that this book will help alert parents to prayer-sharing occasions so that its last page will be but a beginning of many "prayers by parents" to a loving heavenly Father.

—Jeanette L. Groth

Special Days

A SUNNY DAY

Dear God, It's a beautiful, sunny day. What a welcome change after all the dreariness and rain. I can tell the difference in my child, Lord. It is like something has awakened within him—a new joy, a new happiness. Lord, help me to guide my child so Your Son will always shine in his heart. Help that Son to make a noticeable difference even on the dreary days of life. Give my child a real source of light and energy to rely on in You. Amen.

FIRST DAY OF SCHOOL

Today's the day, dear Jesus. It's my child's first day of school. We both have butterflies. Now some of the values and ideas I've taught will be put to the test. Be with my child. Remind her that she is Your child. Be with the teacher that he/she will guide my child well. Help me to be a supportive parent so that we can be partners in raising this child to bring glory to Your name. Amen.

A BAPTISM

Dear Lord, today we saw a Baptism in church. What a beautiful time for me to remind my child that he, too, was baptized. I want this knowledge to be so much a part of his life. I want him to remember that he is Your child. When he is lonely, let that be his comfort. When he is afraid, let his baptism reassure him of Your presence. When he feels guilty, let his baptism remind him of Your forgiveness. When he is joyful, let him be reminded of the true source of all joy—Your love. Amen.

BIRTHDAY

Today is birthday day, holy Father. How quickly time progresses. I remember the day I first saw this child that You have entrusted to me. Now we've shared some days and experiences together. Help me guide this child well. May Your Holy Spirit bless me with wisdom and understanding to impart Your knowledge and ways in a manner that will last for all eternity. Keep my child's faith alive and growing. Give me Your blessing that each birthday will bring us always closer to You. Amen.

ADVENT

Dear Jesus, it's Advent. Each day as my child opens another window on the Advent calendar we talk about Christmas coming. We talk about Your lowly birth. Impatiently my child asks, "Now how many days until Christmas?" Lord, teach me to prepare my child for Your second coming. Help me to keep her close to You and always waiting for You. As we wait, Lord Jesus, keep us busy doing Your will. Amen.

CHRISTMAS

It's Christmas, dear Father. We've planned, decorated, and waited. We've read the Christmas story from Your Word. Now the excitement is mounting. We sense the joy the shepherds felt as they heard the news of their newborn Savior. Help my child to know the greatness of Your gift to us. Let us kneel before the manger with joy and thanksgiving over the humble birth of Your Son. Amen.

VALENTINES

We made Valentines today, Lord. How much fun it is to cut and glue and once again tell others that we love them. Lord, as Christians let that be an everyday event for us. Let me be quick to tell my child and those I love how much they mean to me. Amen.

EASTER

It's Easter, Jesus. We've enjoyed new clothes, colored eggs, the lilies, and our worship at church. Oh, how hard it is to keep the world from crowding in on the importance of this day. Let things take second place for my child, Lord. Let him know the real Easter joy that comes from knowing that You died for us and rose again. As our family shares that story together, let it stir our hearts so that Easter will be a part of our everyday living. Amen.

FIRST DAY OF SUNDAY SCHOOL

It's my child's first day of Sunday school. How thankful I am for Your church, heavenly Father. Through its fellowship I have partners to help me guide my child and teach her Your Word. Help my child's heart be receptive to Your Word. Help her to listen and put Your Word into action in her life. Amen.

A SPRING DAY

It's spring, Lord. As my child and I walk we have observed the new awakening of Your creation. My child is amazed to see grass after the long winter of snow. Each flower and budding tree is a marvel. O God, once again Your creation speaks to us. Help me to point out to my child how Your renewed world reminds us of Your love and our own awakening in the Resurrection. Help me to talk freely of our death and the new life which Your Son Jesus Christ has won for us. Send Your Holy Spirit to us so that my child can grow up confident of the sure hope of life eternal. Amen.

Special Needs

FORGIVENESS

I've made the wrong decision, God. I'm just WRONG! Help me to be a big enough person to tell my child that I'm sorry. Let her see me not as someone who is perfect, but as someone who is leaning hard on Your love and forgiveness. Now, eternal Father, let me feel reassured of Your forgiveness through Christ Jesus. I am sorry. Amen.

ILLNESS

My child is ill, Lord. Oh, maybe it is just a cold, but it still makes me wish for the impish, orneriness of yesterday. Help me as I pray with him to help him realize that he can trust even these little hurts to You. You care for him and love him as one of Your own; You have the power to make him better. Give me patience with his grouchiness, and help me be kind and understanding. Amen.

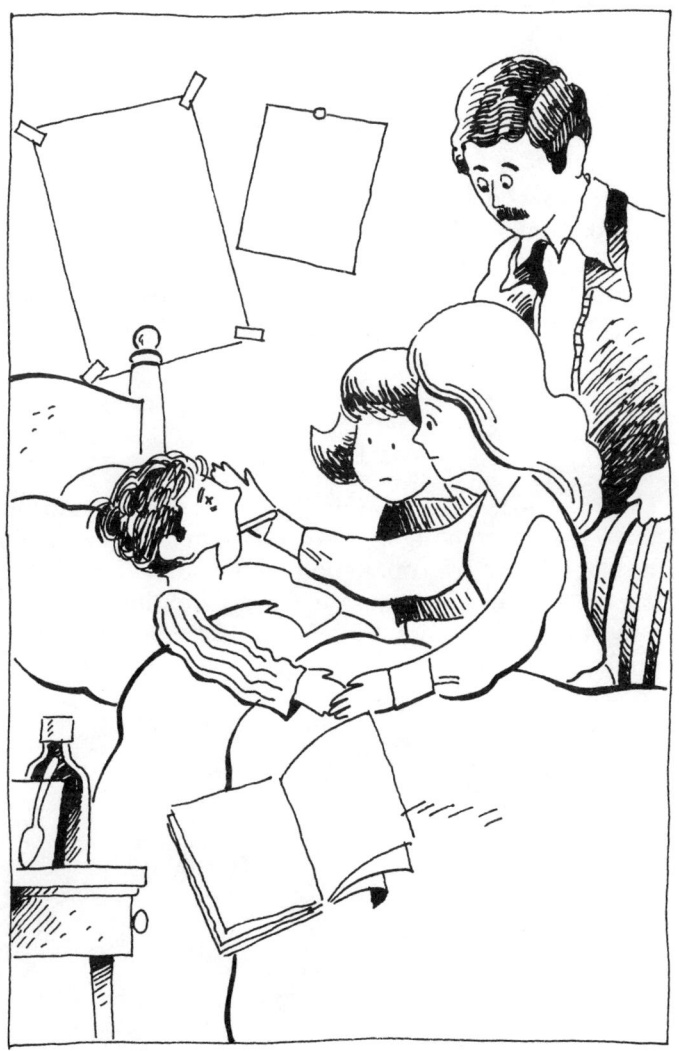

ILLNESS

My child is sick, Lord. It hurts to see her so lifeless and upset. Now I'd love to see that extra energy I sometimes dread. Lord, we've prayed together for Your healing. Help my child know You are with her and that all healing comes from You. Guide the doctor's skills so that soon we can thank You for the blessing of renewed health. Amen.

COUNSEL

How do I do it, Lord? How do I find ways to explain to my child that even though "Everybody is doing it," it is not right for us. We are Your people, and in some respects we are set apart and different. Help me to show her that Your ways bring true happiness and not just momentary joy. Amen.

PATIENCE

Dear Father, give me patience. As Your erring child I see that You are so often patient with me. We've been working on toilet training, and our successes are small compared with our failures. Forgive my quick disgust and help me place this small aspect of learning in the proper perspective. Help me to be quick to praise success and full of understanding for failure. Amen.

WAITING

We're waiting, Jesus. My child must have been to the window 10 times in the last hour. Grandma and grandpa are coming, and happiness and anticipation are the order of the day. We've prepared for them. The bed is made, the dinner is cooked, and we're more than ready. O Savior, we're waiting. We're waiting for You to come again. Help us to be ready. Help me teach my child to watch and wait for You. Let us prepare our hearts so that You'll find us joyfully ready at Your final return. Amen.

The World Around Us

VACATION

We're going on vacation, Lord. Help us to remember it is not a vacation from You. Let the things we see and do give me new opportunities to talk to my child and help me to teach her more of You. Remind me to ascribe the beauty that we see, the fun we have, the closeness we share, to You and Your gracious gifts. Be with us so that we will be safe from harm as we travel. Keep our home and loved ones safe while we are away from them. Amen.

THE PARK

We played in the park today, Lord. It was fun to see the children play together without any inhibitions. They didn't even notice the differences in their skin, their hair, their clothing. All they knew was that they were having a good time. Help me to teach my children that such differences do not matter. Help me to remind them of the unity we share as children of a loving heavenly Father, who sent His only Son to win for us eternal life. Amen.

SNOW

It snowed! My child is ecstatic. White has covered everything. The trees sparkle with their new covering. The dirtiness of yesterday is gone. Help me to teach my child that this is the way Your forgiveness covers our many sins. You see them no more because Your Son Jesus Christ gave His life for us. You only see the whiteness of redemption that He has given us. Amen.

THE ZOO

We've just come from the zoo, Lord. We've laughed at the monkeys, fed the deer, and intently watched the dolphins perform. My child has squealed with delight! What a wonderful God You are! I, too, want to exclaim with delight over Your goodness and the marvels of Your creation. You've created such a variety in Your world for us to enjoy. Help us to also care for and be responsible for the creation You have given us so that future children will also enjoy the full spectrum of Your diverse universe. Amen.

THE FISH

Dear Jesus, our fish died. It was a small part of Your creation, but it was important to my child. It gave us a chance to talk of death, not in a scary way but as a part of life that You have shared and conquered for us. Help my child to know that we need not fear death because of the gift of eternal life You have won for us. Help him to look forward to the joys of life in heaven with You. Amen.

Thanks For . . .

RETURNED HEALTH

Thank You, Lord, for making my child feel better. Now we're going to say "thank You" together to You. I want my child to see that prayers are answered. Help me to use the opportunities I have so often to point out Your answers to our prayers. Give us a true sense of thankfulness for the many gifts You have given us. Especially today, thank You for doctors, nurses, medicine, and Your wonderful healing hand. Amen.

JESUS PICTURE

Jesus, thank You for artists that draw pictures of You. My child already feels that You are kind and loving from the picture in his room that shows You blessing the little children. Thank You that through these pictures I have opportunities to tell my child more of the stories about You. Help me to find a variety of ways to increase his knowledge of You. Amen.

SKILLS

My child has mastered cutting, Lord. It's just a beginning of the long line of skills she'll need to live in this world. Thank You, God, for my child's muscular skills, sight, and coordination. Thank You for the patience You have given her to keep working at a task until she masters it. May she always use all her skills as ways to serve You. Amen.

SIMPLE GIFTS

A pencil and paper are such simple things, good Father. It amazes me that they can entertain my child for such a length of time. Thank You for such simple gifts. Thank You for creative minds that help us draw, design, and discover such interesting things. Amen.

GROWTH

I'm putting away clothes, Lord. It seems it was just yesterday that all these things fit. Now the slacks are three inches too short and long sleeves have miraculously changed to three-quarter-length ones. Oh, the miracle of growth! Thank You, God, for healthy bodies that do grow. Thank You for healthy minds that can stretch to accommodate new knowledge each day. Help me to find ways to teach my children that we can *always* grow, for our knowledge of You is never complete. Keep my child and me growing, Lord. Amen.

Daily Situations

BATH TIME

Bath time, Lord. Thank You for the simple joys we so often take for granted. Thank You for warm water, bath toys, soap, and fluffy towels. As I help my child clean the externals, send Your Holy Spirit to help me to teach him about cleanliness on the inside and about Your love for us. Help me find ways to guide his thoughts so that they too remain clean and pure and centered on You. Amen.

FAMILY DEVOTIONS

Thank You, dear God, for family devotions. It is a beautiful time that we sit at Your feet and share from Your Word. Thank You that You speak so clearly to us. Thank You for materials that lead us and guide us to a closer understanding of You and Your will. Amen.

NAP TIME

It's nap time. Who needs it worse, the children or me? Thank You, Father, for rest that refreshes us, that gives us new patience, that rebuilds us. Thank You for those pauses that give us time to reflect, reevaluate, and regroup our forces. Thank You for quiet and for Your constant presence. Amen.

A CHILD'S DANCE

Today I watched my child dance with glee and reckless abandon to a mighty version of the "Hallelujah Chorus," Lord. As the rich strains built, so did my child's joy. I suppose there would be some who would be shocked to think of dancing to such a sacred work, and yet for this small child it seemed so right. What else could express his happiness, his inner joy. Oh, help me, Lord, not to stifle the joy he has in Jesus. Send Your Holy Spirit that I may guide my child to see the fullness of joy and express it to You. Amen.

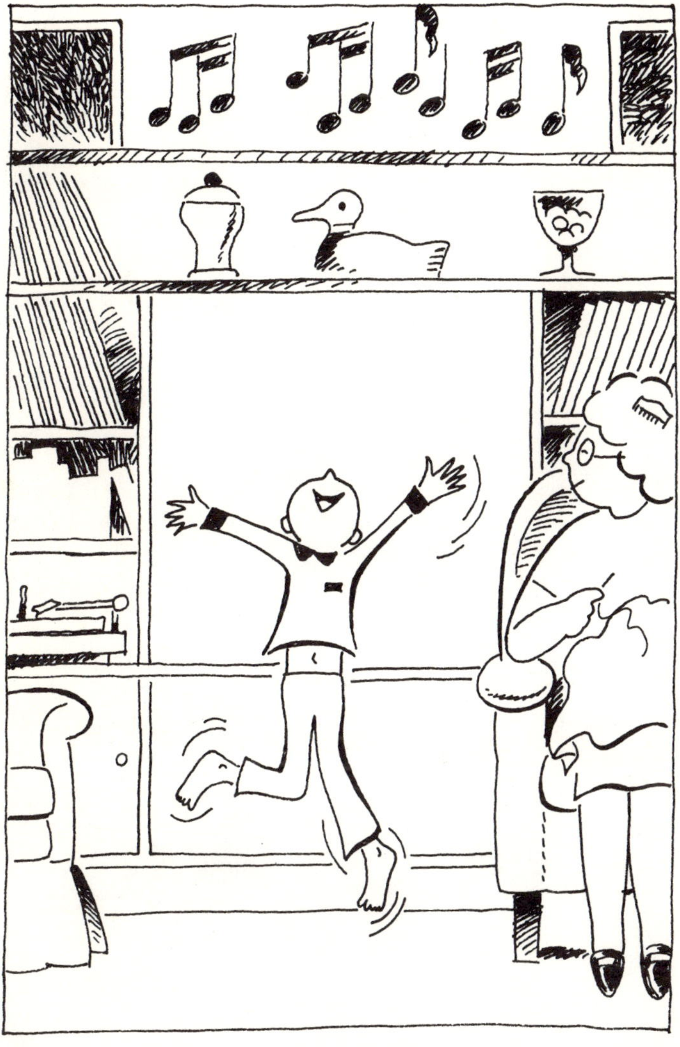

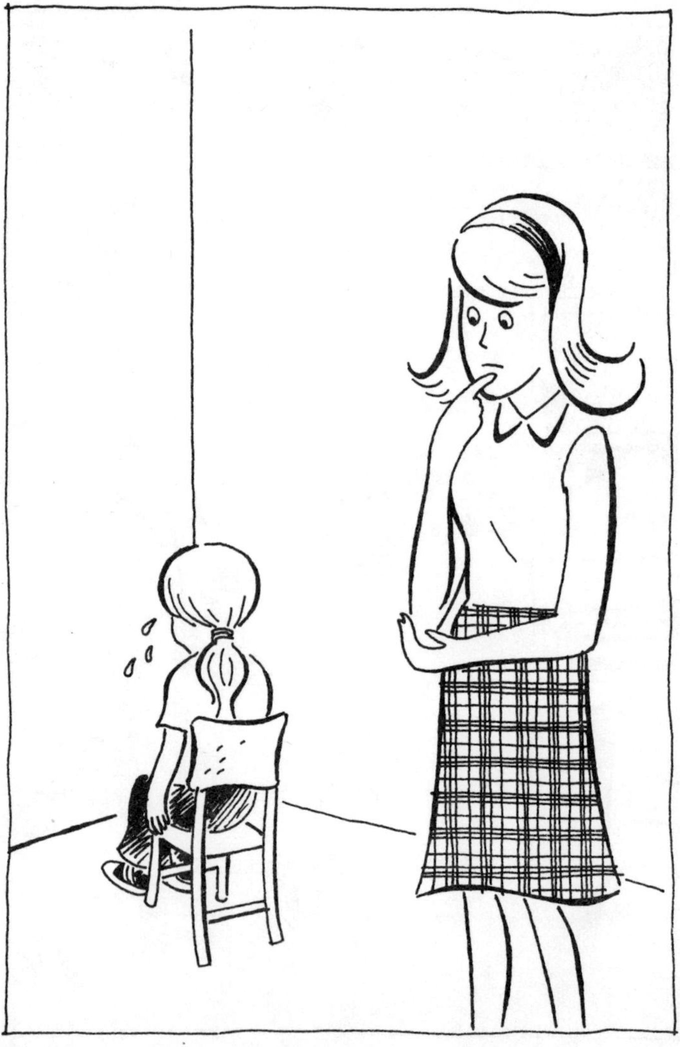

DISCIPLINING

I just disciplined my child, Lord. It hurts me, but I don't want that action to persist. I know she thinks that I'm angry with her. Soon she'll want a hug to reassure her that all is well and that I still love her. I'm always ready to show that. Thank You, God, for disciplining me and for showing me Your saving grace. Thank You for keeping me close to You and constantly reassuring me that even in the rough times You love and care for me because I have been redeemed by the offering of Your Son Jesus. Amen.

HIDING

Hiding is a favorite game these days. It is funny to see my child hide in places that are so obvious to me. Oh, Lord, it is almost the same when we, Your children, try to hide from You. You see us. How obvious our tactics are. Help me always to know that I'm really out in the open with You. Let this be a comfort to me for I can always seek Your help and know You are there. Amen.

QUESTION

"Do you believe in God, Mom?" What a question! O Lord, put the right words in my mouth. Let me use this opportunity to once again share with my child the beautiful friendship that I share with You. I want him to see that You are more than a story or historical event to me. I want him to know that I count on You as *my* Savior and *my* God. Give me the words that will help me share what it means to have a personal, living relationship with You. Amen.

TV VIEWING

We've just watched our favorite television show, Lord. Help me use this medium wisely. Help me to be selective in viewing so that what we see will reinforce Your will. Help me to use the programs that we watch together as springboards to discussion that will help us grow as a Christian family. Amen.

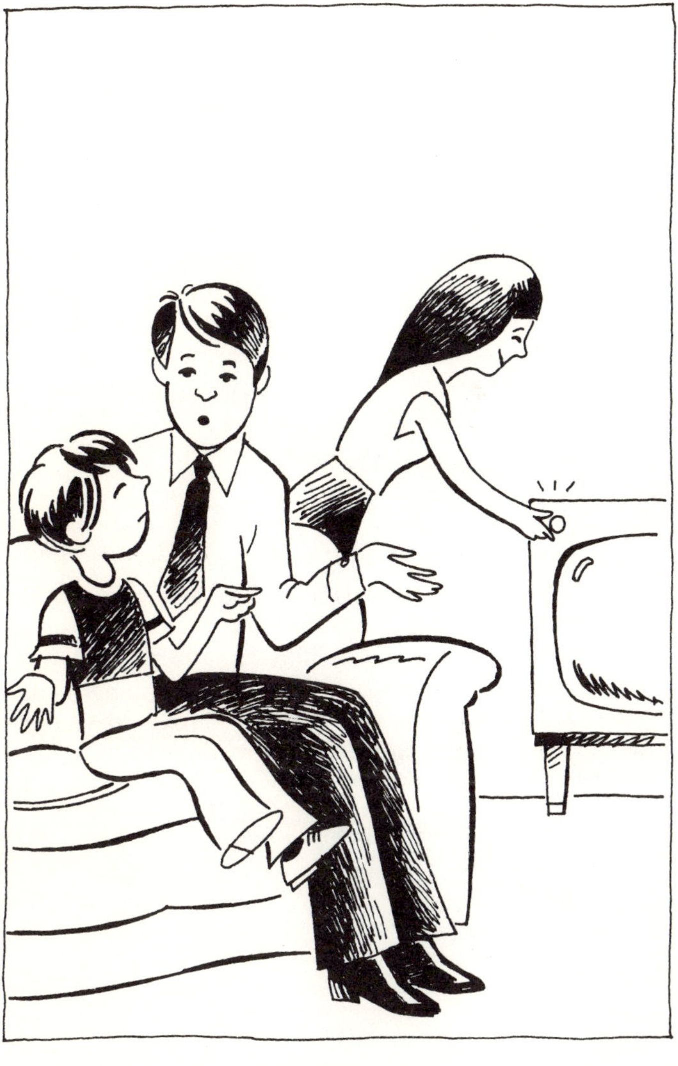

FAVORITE SHOWS

We've just watched a favorite television show, dear Father. How much my child learns from those funny characters. Help me to guide my child's viewing so that her mind is filled with thoughts and ideas that would be acceptable to You. Help me through Your Holy Spirit to discuss freely what we view together so that through this medium we may grow as Christians in our ideas and attitudes. Amen.

SUPPER

We're trying something new for supper, Lord. My child is doubtful of this new food. Help me to teach him a sense of adventure as he approaches even such a small part of the unknown. Help me to teach him that new doesn't mean bad if it is from You and a part of Your plan. Help my child be ready to broaden his horizons and constantly expand his world to see Your grace and the many good things that come from Your loving hand. Amen.

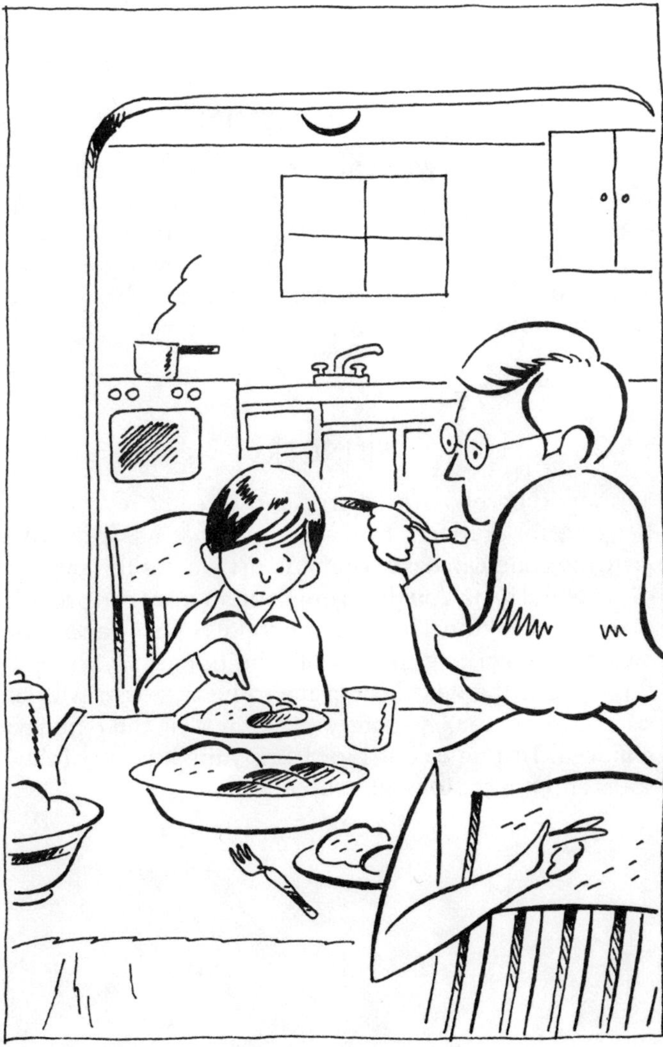

DISAGREEMENTS

How do You teach gentleness, dear Jesus? The pushing at play makes me cringe. The quick fist or sudden angry slap makes me feel so perplexed. O God, help me to be more gentle. Let the Holy Spirit pour the gentleness of Your love through me so that my child will see that might and force do not make right in Your eyes. Amen.

HUNGER

Supper is barely over, Lord, and already my child is begging for a snack. It is amazing what an appetite a growing child can have. Thank You, God, for this miracle of growth. Thank You that from Your bounty I can provide plenty of nutritional food for my child. Help me also to be aware and working to alleviate the hunger of children throughout the world. Help me to be a partner with all parents who seek to satisfy the needs of their hungry children. Through Your Word satisfy the hunger of their souls and the souls of all people. Amen.

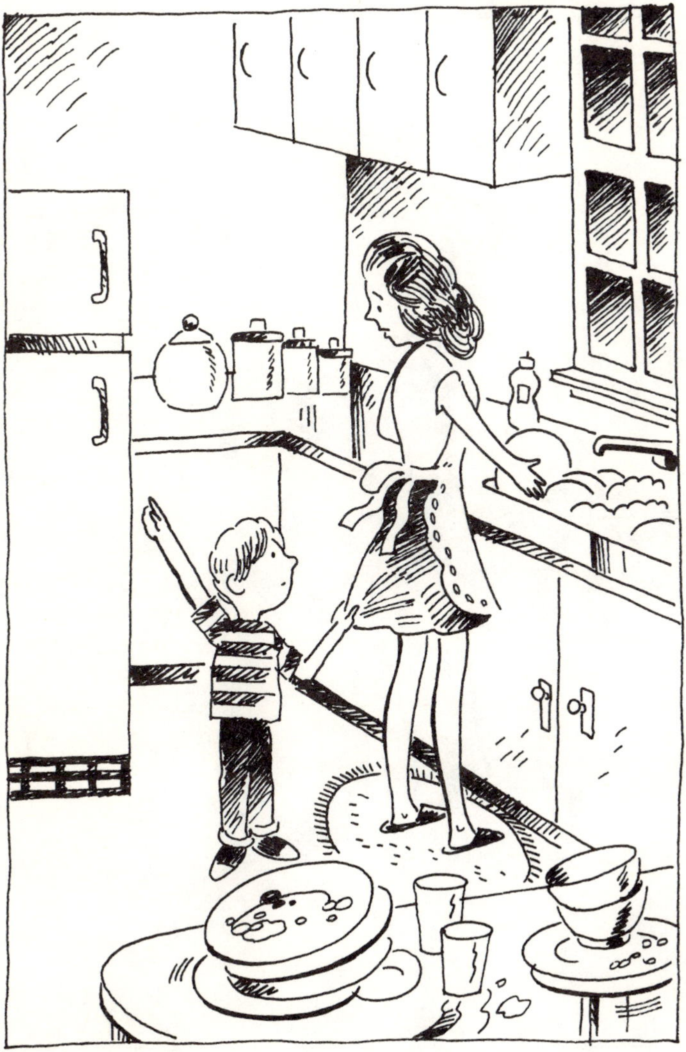

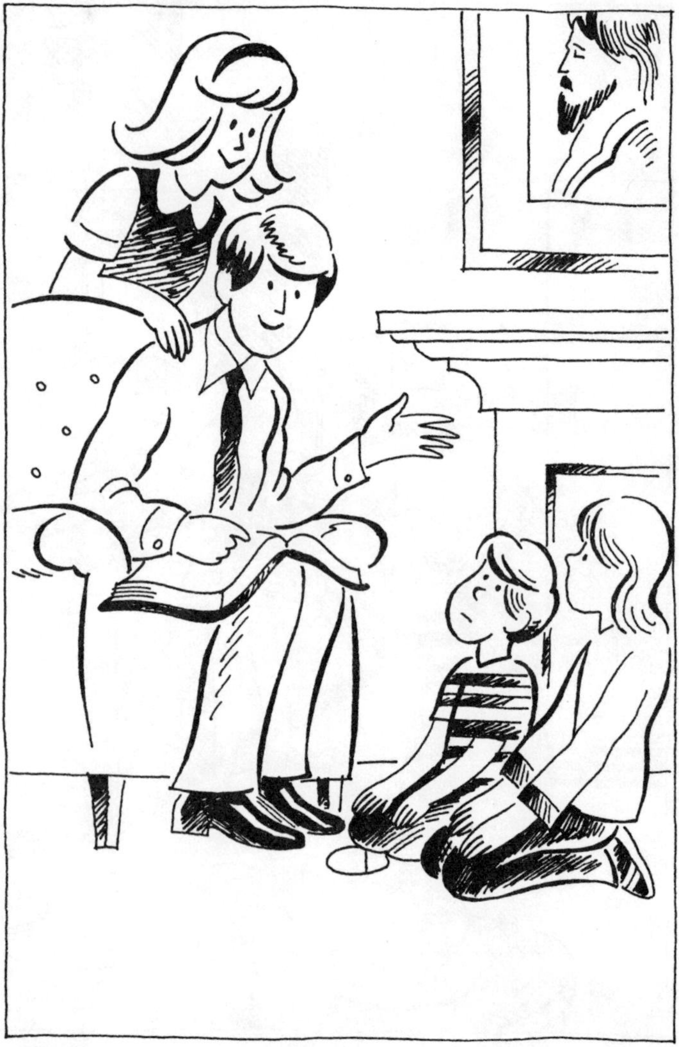

DEVOTIONS

We've just had our devotions, heavenly Father. I'm amazed at all the little details a child can remember. Help us to continue to study Your Word. Sometimes it is a temptation to say, "I'm too tired" or "I'm too busy." Let me see the value of studying Your Word together so that it will be a top priority in my life. What a joy to see my child intent on Your Word. Help him and me to see Your Son Jesus Christ on every page. Amen.

PRAYER

A simple prayer from a child must cause You much joy, gentle Shepherd. Day by day my child has worked hard to master that prayer. I want her to find many ways and words to use to talk to You. May You always be her best friend. Amen.

LOVE

O God, how empty love would be if it were not founded on Your love. So, Lord, I want to tell You again—I love You. Thank You for loving me. Amen.

FAMILY

Our family is together, Lord. Thank You for this circle of people that have established a rich heritage for my child. Let him always feel a special warmth and love from these people. Let him bring honor to our name and Your name by his godly life. Bless this family that has been won for You through the victory of our Savior Jesus Christ. Let us accept the differences in our family but unite, together with all Christians, under our oneness in You. Amen.

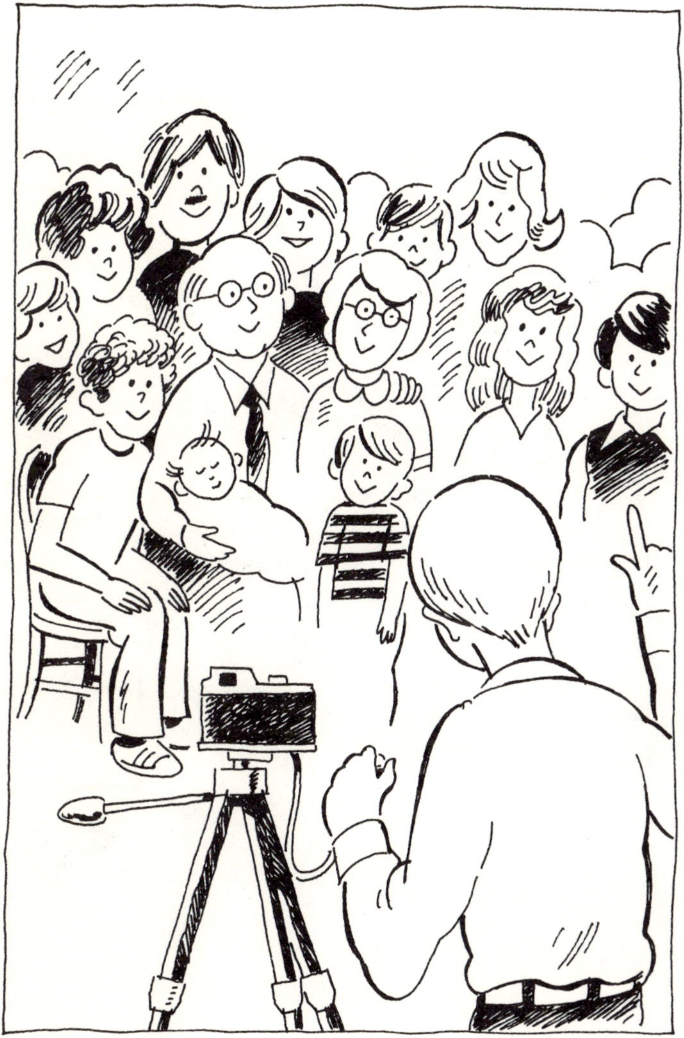

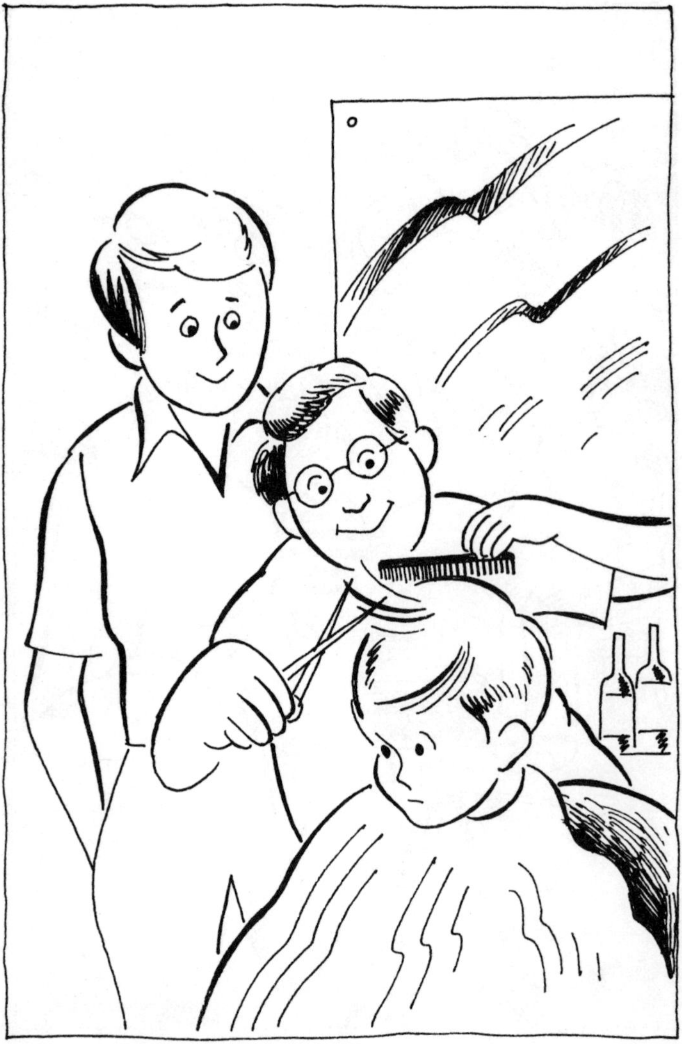

THE HAIRCUT

My child just had a haircut, Lord. When I see the hair on the floor, I am reminded of Your words that You know the very number of hairs on our heads. I am thankful that You are concerned with the small things of our life, dear Father. I know that nothing is so trivial or unimportant that I cannot share it with You and know that You care about it. Help me to remind my child of Your constant interest in him so that he, too, will share things large or small freely with You. Amen.

DADDY IS GONE

Dear Father in heaven, our daddy is gone on a business trip. How much my child misses him. He asks where he is and even sets his place at mealtime. Keep him safe, Lord. Let him know what an important part he is of our family. Guard him from danger as he travels, and return him safely to our family circle. Amen.

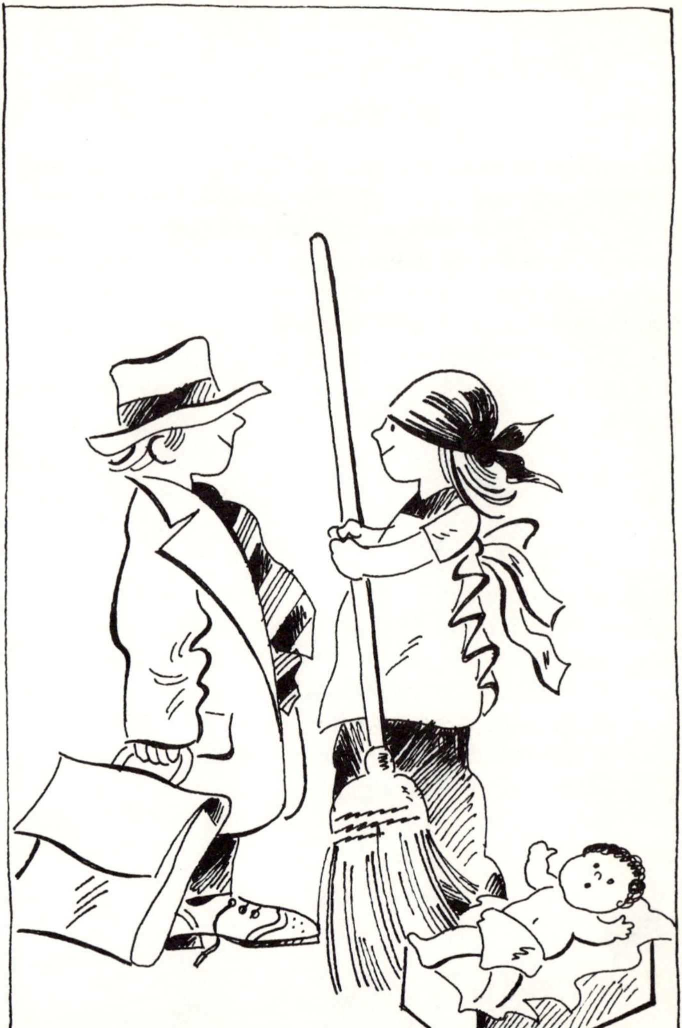

PLAYING HOUSE

My children are playing house, Lord. It is fun to see the roles so accurately enacted. They've chosen quickly who will be the mother, father, and baby brother. Lord, they sow the seeds of so many future decisions. It seems so far in the future that they will choose real lifetime roles. Help them to make decisions that will bring glory to Your name and happiness to their lives. Help them to find Christian companions and spouses who will help them build their lives with You as the center. Amen.

THE FUNERAL

My child attended his first funeral, dear Lord. It wasn't a close friend, so it was a good time to go without feeling a deep sense of loss while becoming aware that death is a part of life. Thank You that in our Christian family the joy of the Resurrection undergirds the sorrow of the moment. Thank You for Your Son Jesus Christ, whose death on the cross made sure our hope of eternal life with You. Help me to answer my child's questions well so that death will not hold fear but the promise of eternal joy. Amen.

Common Objects

CRAYONS

Dear God, we're picking up the crayons again. I can't help noticing the variety of colors. It reminds me of the beautiful colors in the creation that You've given us. Help me to make my child aware of the beauty of the world around us. Help me to call his attention to the tiny spring flowers, the changing leaves, and the lacy snowflakes. Then as we appreciate Your creation, let us be drawn always closer to You, the Creator. Amen.

TOYS

The toys are scattered everywhere, Lord. It seems I've picked them up a thousand times today. Teach me patience. Let me be thankful for these gifts that help my child develop skills, talents, and abilities. Help my child to use her fullest potential so that she may serve You well. Amen.

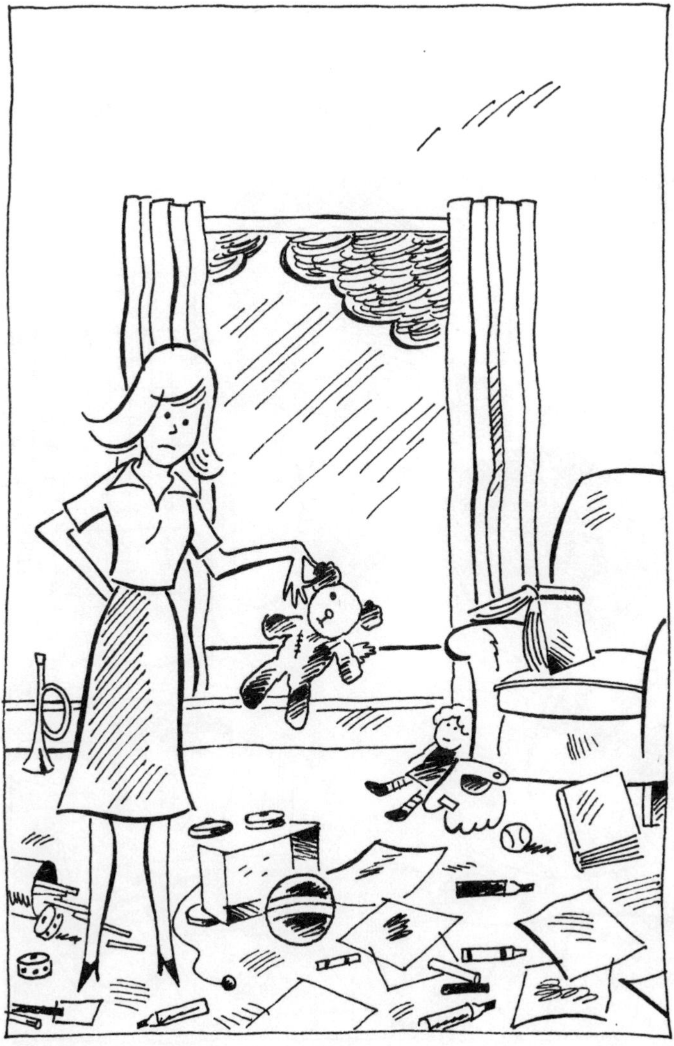

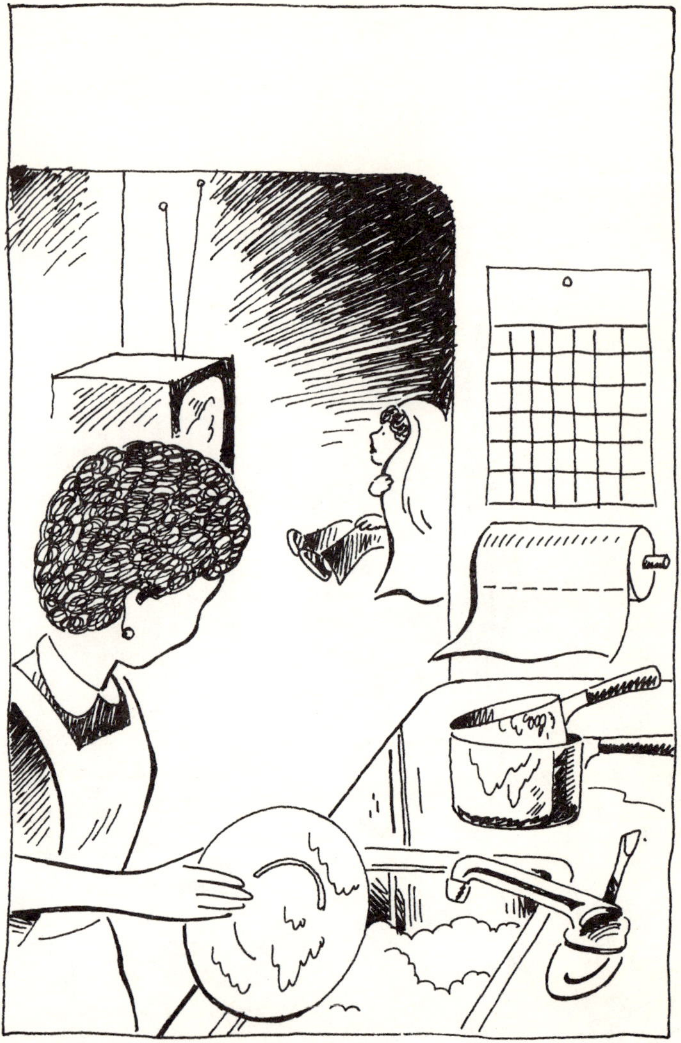

THAT BLANKET

Oh, that blanket. No rest without it. In a strange place it gives security. It can even calm a hurt and catch a tear. I guess we all have *things* that help us feel secure. Help me to teach my child that the real source of security is knowing You, dear Jesus, as mighty Savior and Redeemer. Amen.

THE MIRROR

It's fun to see our reflection in the mirror, Lord. I think my child is just beginning to realize that he is seeing himself and not some other baby making faces at him. When we see our reflection we always see some things we do not like. Help me to teach my child to examine his inner reflection. Let him see his faults and use Your power to improve. Let his beauty be an inner good which shines through to make a beautiful self for the world to see. Amen.

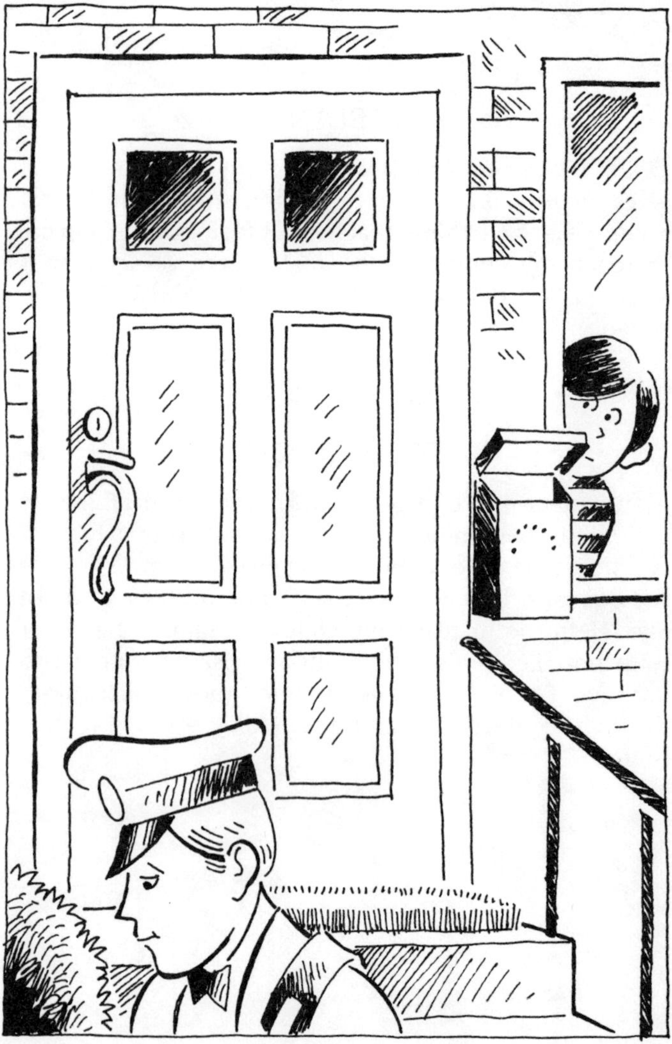

THE MAILBOX

What disappointment! Once again the mailbox is empty. My child has been waiting, not too patiently, each day for the word that her magazine subscription will soon begin. Thank You, Father, that Your Word is always close at hand. When we need a word from You, we can quickly turn to our Bibles and find comfort, joy, and hope. Help me to teach my child a true love for Your Word so that it will be her constant reference. In Jesus' name. Amen.

A SIREN

A siren is blowing. My child is already asking with a frightened look, "Mom, what is that?" I want to explain those sirens, God. I want her to know that they are a sign that people are responding to emergencies. I want her to feel a real concern for those around us who are in trouble. Now, Lord, we pray together, "Dear Jesus, help whoever needs Your help. Be with the policemen, firemen, or ambulance drivers as they help others. Amen." Perhaps now, Lord, as my child hears that siren, she'll think of the help You can give and call on You. Amen.

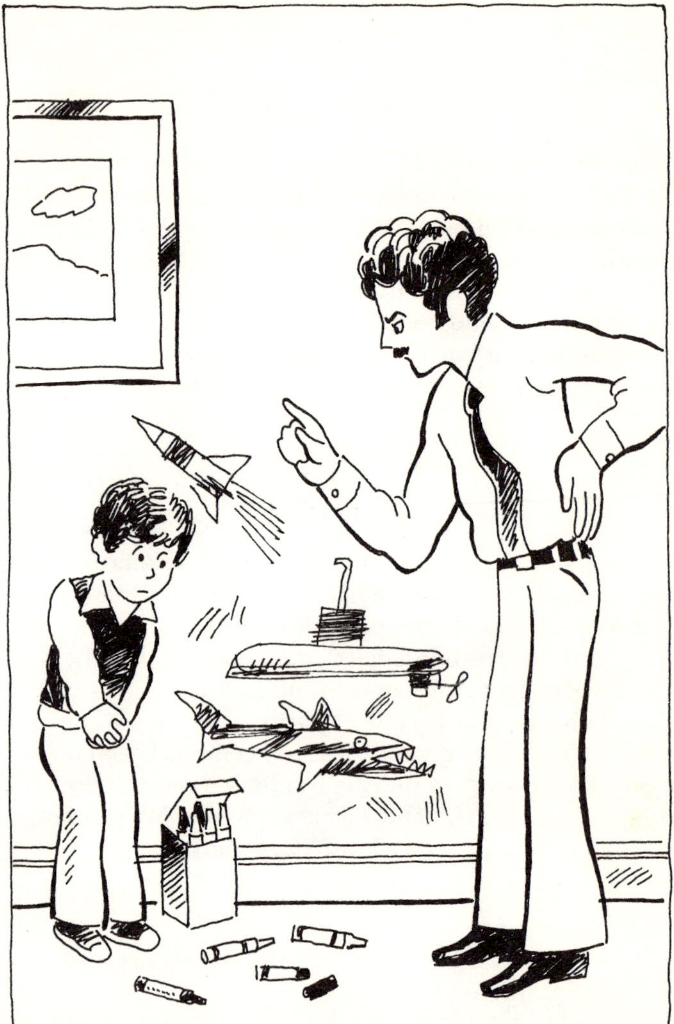

THE WALL

Our wall is marred, Lord. The crayons were too tempting! Now I feel disgust over the extra work that my child has made for me. Lord, how often You must feel disgust as we go against Your will and mar our lives. Forgive us for the messes we make of things. Send Your Holy Spirit and help my child and me do Your will. Give us the joy that comes from following Your Word. Amen.